LET'S-READ-AND-FIND-OUT SCIENCE®

STAGE 2

Coral Reef

by Wendy Pfeffer

illustrated by Steve Jenkins

Collins
An Imprint of HarperCollinsPublishers

With thanks for so generously sharing their expertise:
Dr. Yair Rosenthal, Professor of Marine Biology at Rutgers University
Patricia Glick, from the National Wildlife Federation's Climate Change and Wildlife Program
Leonard Muscatine, from the Department of Zoology at the University of California, Los Angeles

The Let's-Read-and-Find-Out Science book series was originated by Dr. Franklyn M. Branley, Astronomer Emeritus and former Chairman of the American Museum–Hayden Planetarium, and was formerly co-edited by him and Dr. Roma Gans, Professor Emeritus of Childhood Education, Teachers College, Columbia University. Text and illustrations for each of the books in the series are checked for accuracy by an expert in the relevant field. For more information about Let's-Read-and-Find-Out Science books, write to HarperCollins Children's Books, 10 East 53rd Street, New York, NY 10022, or visit our website at www.letsreadandfindout.com.

Library of Congress Cataloging-in-Publication Data

Pfeffer, Wendy.

Life in a coral reef / by Wendy Pfeffer ; illustrated by Steve Jenkins. — 1st ed.

p. cm. — (Let's-read-and-find out science. Stage 2)

ISBN 978-0-06-445222-9 (pbk. bdg.) — ISBN 978-0-06-029553-0 (trade bdg.)

1. Coral reef animals—Juvenile literature. 2. Coral reef ecology—Juvenile literature. I. Jenkins, Steve, date ill. II. Title. III. Series.

QL125.P477 2009   2008000498   591.77'89—dc22   CIP   AC

Typography by Rachel Zegar
09 10 11 12 13 SCP 10 9 8 7 6 5 4 3 2 1

❖

First Edition

For Tim and Jaime, who enjoy
snorkeling over Caribbean reefs
—W.P.

For Jamie
—S.J.

As morning sunbeams stream down through clear blue-green water, a coral reef, built of limestone from tiny sea animals, becomes a magical place.

A coral reef overflows with underwater life. More sea creatures find food and shelter in coral reefs than in any other ocean habitat.

The Great Barrier Reef, a world of wonder off the coast of Australia, is more than 1,200 miles long, the distance from Maine to Florida.

The largest coral reef in the world, it
began forming millions of years ago.

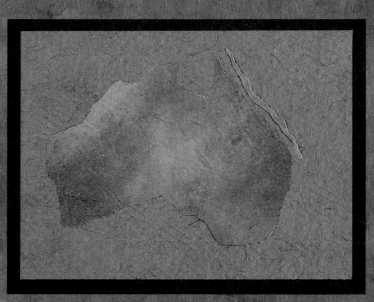

It's hard to believe that all coral reefs, large or small, are built by tiny sea animals called coral polyps, each the size of a grain of rice.

In clear, shallow ocean water warmed by the sun, these tiny tube-shaped coral animals attach themselves to the skeletons of dead coral polyps. Layer upon layer of old coral polyps form beautiful coral reefs.

Other animals keep the reef sturdy. Sea cucumbers spit out the sand they cannot eat, which fills the cracks and crevices in the reef.

This makes the reef stronger so wave action doesn't tumble and crumble it.

Two kinds of coral animals, hard coral polyps and soft coral polyps, live in colonies on the reef.

Hard coral colonies look like boulders, pillars, cactuses, elk horns, or even brains.

Soft coral colonies
look like fans, fingers,
flowers, bits of lovely lace,
or multicolored swaying sea
feathers.
   Hard corals are reef builders.
   Soft corals are reef decorators.
Their rainbow colors give the
reef its beauty.

In this coral kingdom, with its stony towers and turrets, some creatures eat one another and some help one another.

A small goby helps keep other fishes clean and healthy. A grouper allows the goby to remove parasites from its mouth. Parasites can make fish sick.

Then the goby moves over to a spotted
moray eel and eats its dead skin.

A clown fish huddles in the pink-tipped poisonous tentacles of the sea anemone. Because the clown fish is immune to the poison, it has a safe place to stay. In return the clown fish keeps the anemone clean by eating its waste.

Not all reef creatures help one another. Predators that eat sea animals swarm the reef looking for food, so many reef creatures must protect themselves.

When a spiny puffer fish swims by, its predator, a ruffle-headed scorpion fish, pulls the puffer into its mouth. Quickly, the puffer inflates. The scorpion fish can't swallow the puffed-up puffer, so it spits it out.

Many reef creatures also use camouflage as protection from predators. When a decorator crab leaves its safe hiding place, it snips off bits of sponge and attaches them to its shell for camouflage. When the crab gets hungry, it eats bits of food that collect on the surface of the sponge.

The four-eye butterfly fish confuses predators
with false eye spots on its tail. Its enemies don't
know which way the butterfly fish is headed.

As the sun sets, the reef's blue-green water looks gray. The reef's day creatures seek safe places to hide as barracuda, snappers, and sharks cruise the reef at night.

23

In the early evening, about a week after a full moon in late spring, coral polyps release pink egg and sperm bundles into the water. They look like an underwater flurry of cherry blossoms.

Later, tiny larvae hatch, float for several days, settle on a hard surface, and then mature into adult coral polyps.

Coral polyps can also reproduce and enlarge a reef by budding. Coral buds grow on coral polyps, just as branches grow on trees.

Around midnight the reef is filled with darkness, as if it were covered with a black blanket. But the reef is just as alive at night as during the day.

Coral polyp tentacles reach out, snatch zooplankton, and sweep them into the coral polyp's mouth.

A flashlight fish, with light pouches under its eyes, attracts the zooplankton that it eats. Flaps of skin let the flashlight fish blink its lights on and off. The lights reflect off orange cup coral that bursts with color as it blooms at night.

The green moray eel stalks fish in the dark by using its sense of smell. But it slips by a parrot fish in a deep sleep. Why?

A colorless liquid oozes from the parrot fish's body and covers it like plastic wrap. The eel can't smell the parrot fish, so it glides right by.

A spiny lobster searches the sandy bottom for clams, mussels, snails, and starfish.

After hunting all night by smelling and touching, an octopus returns to its cave at first light, and coral polyps withdraw their tentacles as a new day begins in the reef.

Find Out More About Coral Reefs

Fun Facts

* Although coral reefs cover less than 1% of Earth's surface, they are home to 25% of all marine fish species.

* Five hundred million people rely on coral reefs for food and jobs.

* Without the coralline structures that support them, parts of Florida would be underwater.

* Organisms found in coral reef environments have been used to help treat many diseases, including cancer, HIV, ulcers, and cardiovascular diseases.

* Coral reefs generate an estimated $375 billion per year around the world in goods and services.

Coral Reefs in Trouble!

* An estimated 25% of coral reefs have already disappeared and an estimated two-thirds of all coral reefs are at risk today.

* If the present rate of destruction continues, 70% of the world's coral reefs will be destroyed by the year 2050.

* Nearly all of the reefs in Southeast Asia—the most species-rich reefs on Earth—are at risk.

* Since 1975, more than 90% of the reefs in the Florida Keys have lost their living coral cover.

*Threats to the world's coral reefs include:
  * Pollution
  * Disease
  * Overfishing
  * Dynamite and cyanide fishing
  * Sedimentation
  * Bleaching caused by rising ocean temperatures
  * Rising levels of acid in seawater due to changes in the atmosphere

Famous Coral Reefs

*The Great Barrier Reef, Queensland, Australia—the largest coral reef system in the world

*The Belize Barrier Reef—the second largest in the world, stretching from southern Quintana Roo, Mexico, and all along the coast of Belize down to the Bay Islands of Honduras

*The New Caledonia Barrier Reef—the second longest double barrier reef in the world; located in the South Pacific, east of Australia

*The Andros Barrier Reef—the third largest in the world, following along the east coast of Andros Island, Bahamas, between Andros and Nassau

*The Red Sea Coral Reef—located off the coast of Egypt and Saudi Arabia

*Pulley Ridge, Florida—the deepest photosynthetic coral reef in the world